DOWN UNDER

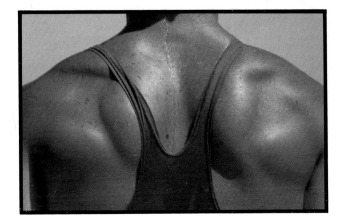

To Rosanne

First published in the United States
by Salem House, 1985. A member
of the Merrimack Publishers' Circle,
47 Pelham Road, Salem NH 03079

This book was designed and produced by
Lansdowne-Rigby International
5 Great James Street
London WC1N 3DA
and adapted from 'Lifesaver' published by
Lansdowne Press, Sydney
a division of RPLA Pty Limited
176 South Creek Road, Dee Why West, NSW, Australia 2099

© Copyright 1985 Peter James

ISBN 0–88162–077–7

Library of Congress Catalog Card Number 84–52306

Designed by Roger Daniels
Captions by Bruce Black
Typeset by Fakenham Photosetting Limited
Printed by New Interlitho S.p.A., Milan

Peter James

Peter James was born in Sydney, Australia in 1947. His interest in swimming began when he was first taught to face the water by his mother, at the Bronte Bogey Hole. He later went on to represent his school, Marcellin College, at swimming.

His interest in lifesaving began with a very personal contact when he was rescued at Bronte Beach, at the tender age of ten. He also remembers the spectacle of the Royal Surf Carnival at Bondi Beach in 1954, and that vivid impression stimulated a lifelong enthusiasm for the colours and movements of lifesavers along the Australian coast.

As a director of photography, he has worked on a number of notable films, Caddie, The Irishman, The Killing of Angel Street, The Wild Duck and Rebel, adapted from a play 'No Names No Pack Thrill'. He has also fulfilled a multitude of commissions both inside and beyond Australia but the surf at Tamarama and Bronte beaches always eventually calls him home.

Acknowledgements

Sir Adrian Curlewis CVO CBE: Life Governor of Surf Life Saving Association of Australia
Gus Staunton MBE and Staff: National Executive Director, SLSAA
Ian Badham: Hon. Aerial Facilities Officer
Terry Kirkpatrick: Hon. Editor, Surf Line
Ernie Davis: Administrator, NSW State Centre
Graham Dick: Publicity Adviser, NSW State Centre
Joan Vaughan: Hon. Assistant Secretary, Sydney Branch

Kevin Murray: Bondi Club Historian
Bob Foster: Bronte, Additional Photos
Frank Nolan: Bronte, Club Historian
Jan Hines and Ralph Clark: North Bondi, Club Historians
David Thomas: Speedo
Linda Slutzin: Art Gallery of NSW, Painting by Charles Meere — 'The Beach'
All Officials and Competitors
Andre Fleuren
Rosanne Andrews-Baxter

DOWN UNDER

Peter James

Salem House

SALEM, NEW HAMPSHIRE

Introduction

Australia today is one of the last remaining outposts for real men, a place where masculinity is genuine and where physical strength is a virtue. And it is the Australian lifesaver — so exquisitely photographed in this book — who best embodies the ideal of full masculinity.

Organised in hundreds of surf clubs, Australian lifesavers stand guard over thousands of miles of some of the world's most beautiful yet dangerous beaches. They have to combat thundering waves and powerful rips that can carry the strongest swimmer out to sea. Sharks, crocodiles, and even water buffalo pose an equally menacing threat, yet over 12,000 people were rescued in one season alone. In Australia, the word lifesaver is not a euphemism, it is a statement of fact.

Peter James photographed these magnificent gladiators of the sea during one of their surf carnivals, a dramatic and competitive gathering that pits the clubs against each other in 'Iron Man' events — a gruelling mixture of sprinting, swimming, and mock rescues.

The men in the pictures are not models and are not necessarily aware of the camera. What might be considered vanity has purpose for them — their nylon briefs are rolled into narrow g-strings not for display but to prevent painful nylon burns caused by strenuous rowing — and their eroticism is all the more appealing because it is natural.

Down Under is proof that there is a place where real men thrive. Call them macho, call them jocks, Australian lifesavers are the answer to every woman's yearnings.

The six man rescue team perform their warm-up before competing in the surf carnival. Every stage shows precision — the high stepping action allows the team to keep in step on the soft sand. The traditional swim suits are not an example of prudish morality: the shoulder straps offer some protection to the body and prevent the suit from being washed off in the savage surf.

Left: Faces distorted with grim determination, an indication of just how competitive the carnival events can be. The 'Iron Man' events test physical strength but with a very definite purpose in mind. One day the same 'test' could be used to save a drowning swimmer. This is the start of the run-swim-run event: run for 200 m, swim for 100 m and run for 200 m, all without stopping and within 8 minutes!

Above: Relaxing and releasing some of that boyish energy. It all helps to build up to the peak of fitness.

Above: The four man Reel and Resuscitation team line up, ready for the tortuous rescue event.

Right: The 'belt-man' powers down the beach, set to do battle with the sea.

Each team member has a vital role. The 'lineman' assists the beltman, battling against the waves, by feeding out the line and preventing any fouling. He also constantly watches the beltman for any signal or sign. The muscular control and strength needed for this traditional method of paying out the life line is obviously considerable.

Left: A crucial time — the beltman is swimming back to shore supporting the victim's head above the water. The line is rolled correctly back onto the reel, ready for the next time.

Above: The linesmen stride into the surf to assist the victim. The formal carrying method prevents any breathing restrictions and exerts no unequal strain on any member of the team. The victim is rushed to the nearest spot of dry land where resuscitation begins.

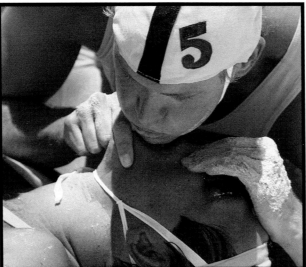

Left: The vital kiss of life, replacing seawater in the lungs with life-giving air.

Above: Speed and team work are essential for success. Here, at the carnival, it is only an exercise, but what these dedicated men are doing could easily be the difference between life and death. Mouth to mouth resuscitation is now universal, but when it was introduced to Australia in 1906, voices of moral indignation were raised. It was thought unseemly that a dying person should have his or her mouth covered by that of a perfect stranger!

Left: The event is over, but the strain and tension are still evident.

The many moods of the competing lifesaver: grim determination illustrates the seriousness and the physical strain — essential ingredients for the competitor; youthful exuberance, showing the carefree pleasure that is part of being a member of this elite band; the unashamed pleasure of looking every bit a real man, even after coming through a gruelling event.

A chance for introspective contemplation about his environment, yet the sea will change from being placid and inviting to rampaging and murderous. The lifesaver loves the sea's many faces.

The rugged, healthy, outdoor Australian look, made all the more appealing and sensuous because it is completely natural. A golden, deep tan contrasts strikingly with blonde hair, bleached by the sun during endless days at the beach.

It is the ambition of every Australian boy to be a lifesaver. They crave for the aura which surrounds these modern day saviours. Children can begin when they are 10 and be an active club member when they are 15.

The surf ski event, a relay exercise for all the team. The ski is larger than a surfboard and has handles for extra grip in rough surf.

Rippling with muscles, tensed up, and ready for action. The lifesaver needs quick reactions, on land and in water.

Proud of their voluntary profession, their clubs, their bodies and their country.

The board rider kneels on the board and paddles with his hands to cut through the waves. The strenuous effort —hence those well developed arm muscles — is rewarded by riding the waves back into shore at speeds of up to 40 miles per hour.

Like native hunters, these two riders expertly steer their surf ski through the breakers. In the competitive events, they race out into open sea, around a buoy and back to shore. The skis are also used for rescue work and provide a platform where resuscitation can be carried out while still in deep water.

The strict formalities of the club board rider are a far cry from the radical image of the 'surfie'. But the 'clubbies' role is important and inviting. A surf carnival can attract over 3,000 competitors.

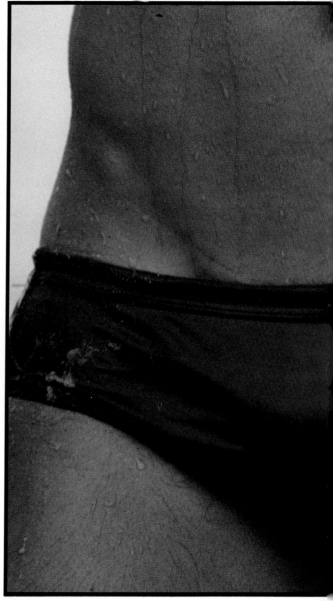

It was not until just before the second world war that men were allowed to go 'topless' on Australian beaches. There were even some swim suits called V shorts, which were worn over the swimming costume in the hope that the two thicknesses of woollen material would disguise the masculine form. It didn't work and thankfully, never caught on.

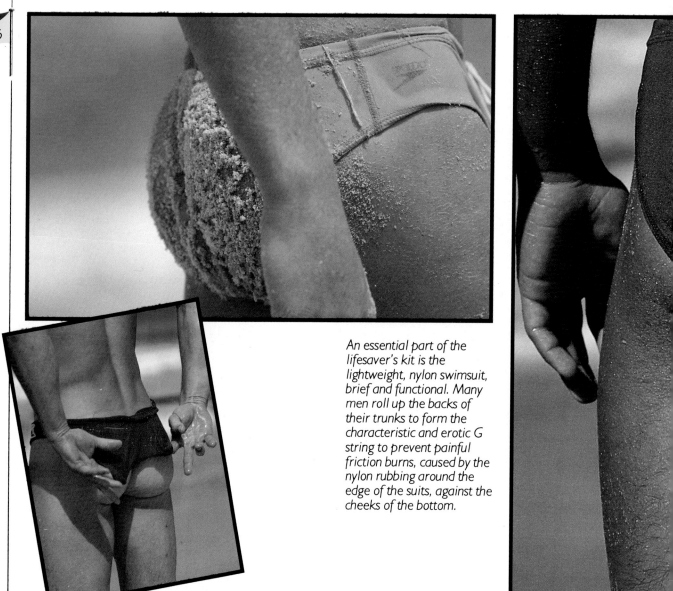

An essential part of the lifesaver's kit is the lightweight, nylon swimsuit, brief and functional. Many men roll up the backs of their trunks to form the characteristic and erotic G string to prevent painful friction burns, caused by the nylon rubbing around the edge of the suits, against the cheeks of the bottom.

The problem of friction burns is especially prevalent with the 'boaties', those brave souls who scythe through the breakers in lightweight rescue boats.

The bronzed five man boat crew prepare to face the savagery of the sea, in the small, lightweight boat. Although they are still a mainstay of the surf carnival, the traditional boats are being replaced for rescue work in some areas by the less elegant, less spectacular, inflatable rubber boats, known as 'rubber duckies'.

The boat race is the most spectacular event in the carnival. The teamwork training is intense and the rivalry amongst the clubs is limitless. The boats are lightly built and easily lifted by the team into the shallow waters.

44

Although this is a
competition, the procedure
and demanding roles of
each person are no different
than the rescue of a
drowning person. It is the
ultimate battle of man.

against the power of the
sea, separated by little
more than a few millimetres
of wood. The strength
needed to row against the
powerful breakers requires
that every muscle is toned
up to the highest degree.

With the boat pushed out into the water, it's all aboard for the four oarsmen and the steersman, called a sweep. His vital task is to steer the boat with a six metre sweep oar from the back of the boat.

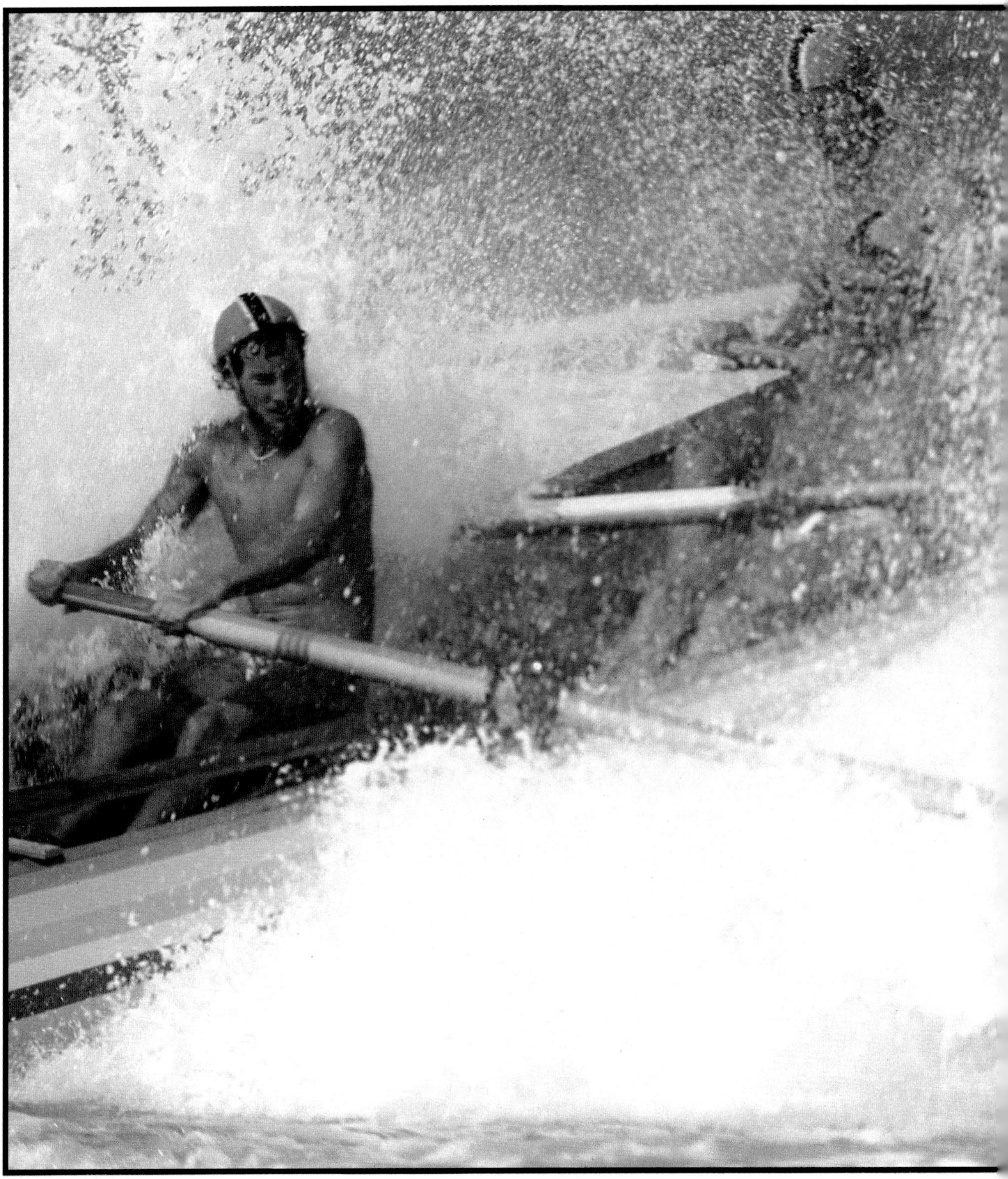

This is the scene that typifies the rugged Australian man: crashing through the thudding breakers with sheer determination. The boats look like a cross between a viking long ship and a ship's lifeboat. The boat race requires the teams to row out into the open sea, around a buoy and then back to shore. Although the waves will speed them on in the journey home, considerable skill is required to prevent the boat from being overturned.

Back to shore and the boat lies erratically angled. The oarsman, physically exhausted, lacks even the smallest amount of energy to release his feet from the foot grips.

The day ends for the boat crew, who return to the shore relaxed and happy at the end of the tough competition.

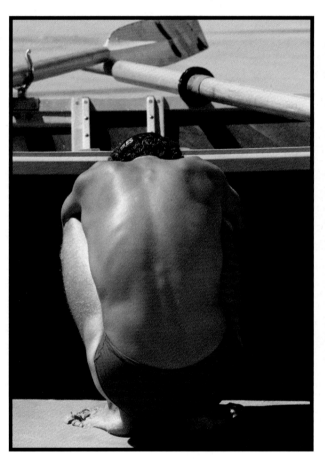

Where it all began, Manly, just a few miles from the centre of Australia's premier city, Sydney. In 1902, one William Gocher challenged the law by swimming during the daylight hours, a pastime that had been previously banned.

Warpaint and weapons of the warriors. The characteristic white nose is sun barrier cream: zinc ointment known affectionately as 'zincie'. It prevents burning under the harsh, relentless sun and it has become a hallmark for those whose lives revolve around the beach.

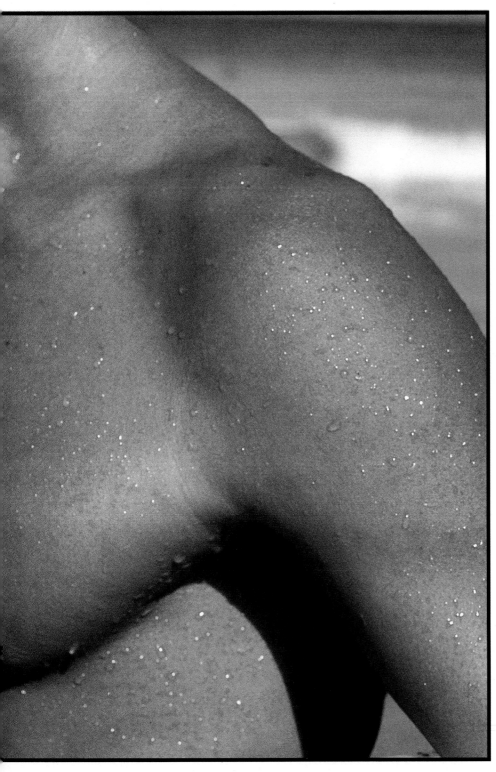

Swimming exercises all the
muscles working the body
into a powerful physique.

Members of the lifesaving clubs are urged to give their all: obligatory patrol duties along the beautiful, but sometimes dangerous, beaches and rigorous training, are seen as the minimum of effort, and the members must make further commitment to retain the lifesavers' exalted position in the eyes of the nation. The commitment must be both physical and mental.

These men are admired for their physical perfection and determined spirits and also for their efforts which are conducted voluntarily. There is no financial reward, except for the occasional gold or silver medal of excellence at the surf carnivals.

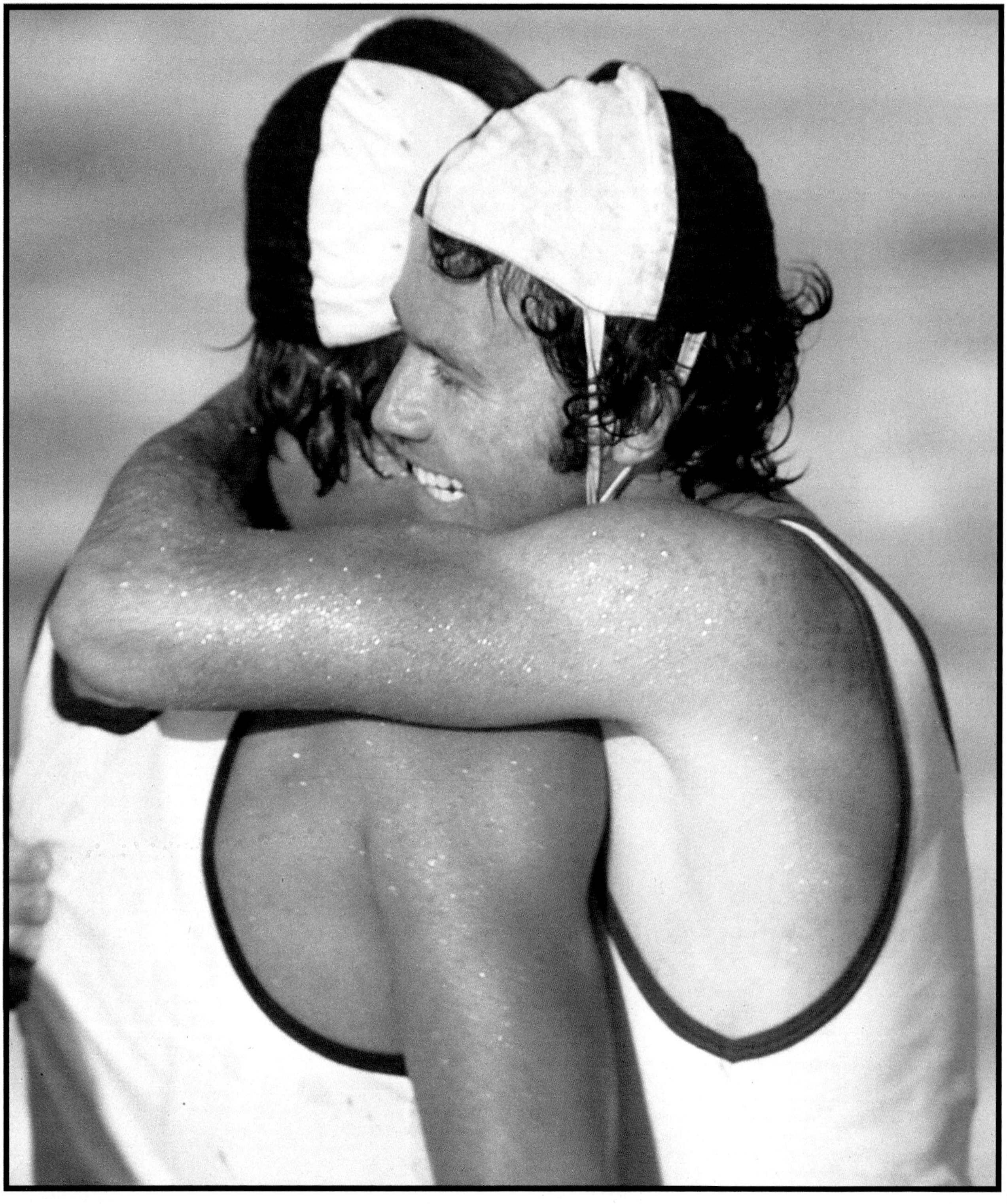

For their efforts in solo
ventures and in team
events, they are rewarded
within the club by an
unbreakable bond of loyalty
to each other. The
companionship is an
essential part of their
activities.

There are other rewards too. The lifesavers are idolised by many. Children see them as a pinnacle of achievement, swimmers feel safe and plenty of beach-goers just like to admire those fine physiques.

Some lifesavers choose clothing in colours which compliment or contrast with their tanned bodies. They select strong colours with sparse, bold designs. There are also ways of adjusting the swim suits to add a touch of individuality.

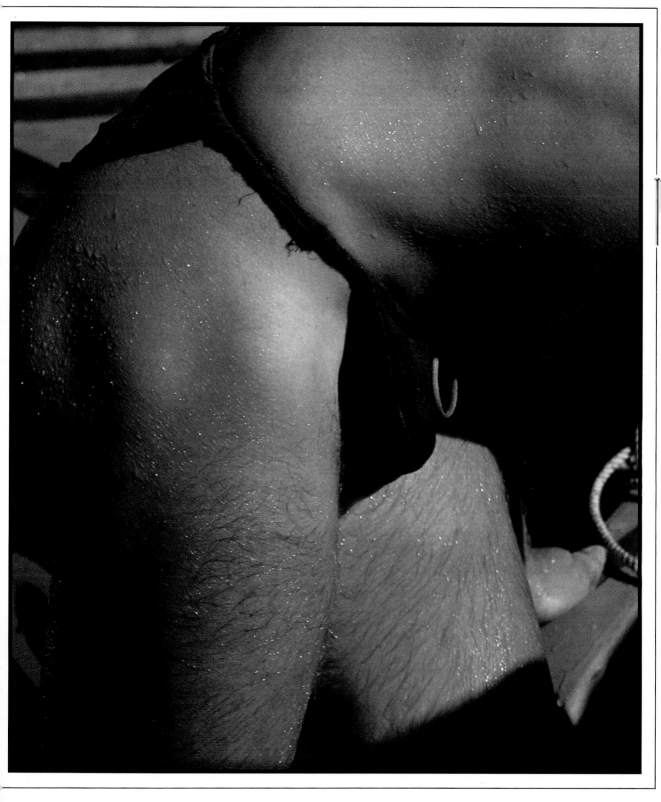

Although the surf carnival
has an element of
entertainment, there is a
serious side — the lifesavers
major task is still concerned
with preserving human life.
In over 230 clubs around
Australia, there are 32,000
members, half of whom are
in active service.

The clean cut image of the lifesaver has been criticised and is not always popular with young Australians, many preferring the individualistic indentity of the 'surfie', imported from America. But since its inception, the *Surf Life Saving Association* has rescued over a quarter of a million victims, many of whom would have surely died if it were not for its efforts. The most dramatic rescue occurred in Sydney in 1938. Four freak waves washed 200 people out to sea and no fewer than 50 life guards saved all but six of them!

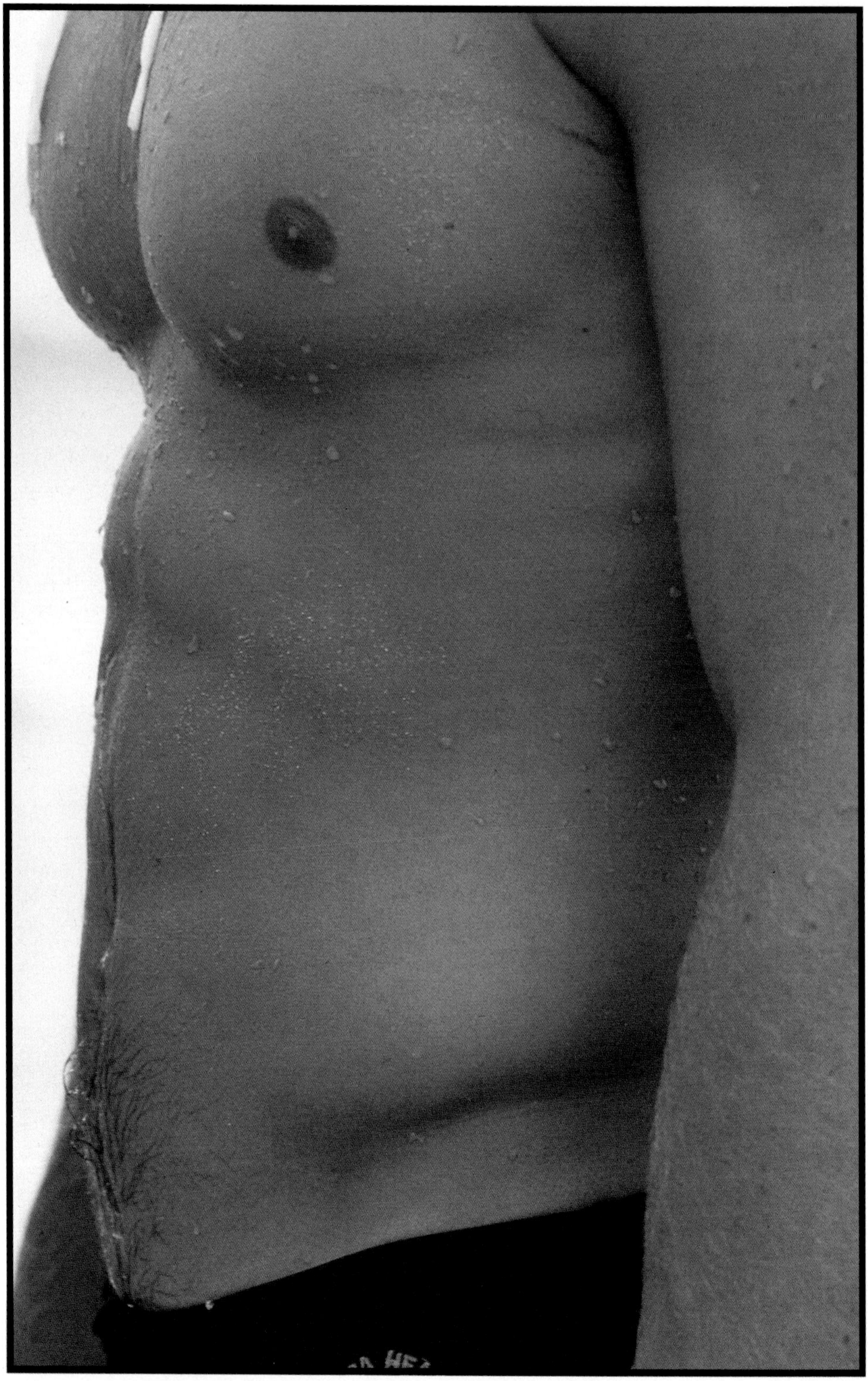

With more people on the beach today, young hopefuls start training at an early age for their Bronze Medallion to indicate the status of lifesaver. Swimming, signalling, reading weather and surf patterns, two way radio operation and six methods of resuscitation must be mastered. And they still have time to look that good!

Training is strict to ensure perfect procedure during the rescues. The young lifesavers are warned of the dangers encountered on the beach, including sun burn, but the sea has worse traps. Besides the rips and the eddies of the sea, lifesavers have to contend with shark attacks, sea snakes and the painful and sometimes fatal stings of jelly fish.

At the weekends, when the
beaches are at their most
crowded, teams of up to
eight lifesavers provide
reassurance and safety for
the swimmers. They patrol
areas marked with flags,
indicating the safe areas to
swim. Characteristic skull
caps identify them and
make them instantly
recognisable in the surf. The
cap also keeps the hair out
of the swimmer's eyes.

80

These men of iron are proficient in not just one of the saving skills, but in all of them. In their rigorous training, they are expected to be part of the Rescue and Resuscitation team, proficient on a surf ski and a competent 'boatie'.

Left: Displays of physical
prowess on beaches attract
admiring stares, but there is
a more serious purpose.
The athletic warm-up
ensures maximum effect
from the muscles. Cramp
can lead to fatal results in
the water.

Above: Nearing the end of
the run-swim-run event,
there is little sign of
strenuous effort needed for
such an exercise.

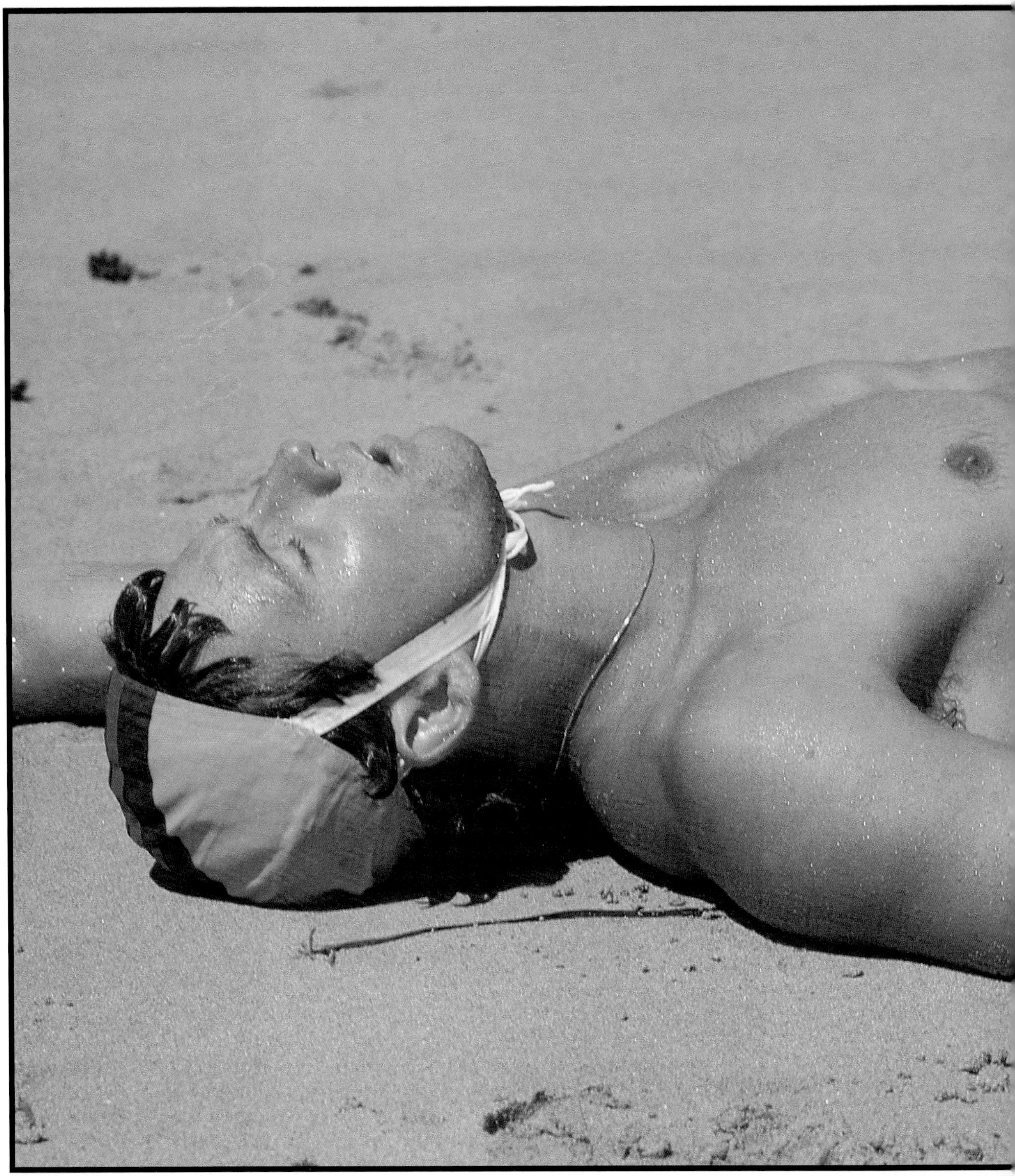

Lifesavers are driven to the limit in efforts to produce their best possible form, whether it be in competition or in a real life drama. The exhaustion at the end produces a welcome sense of relief and achievement.

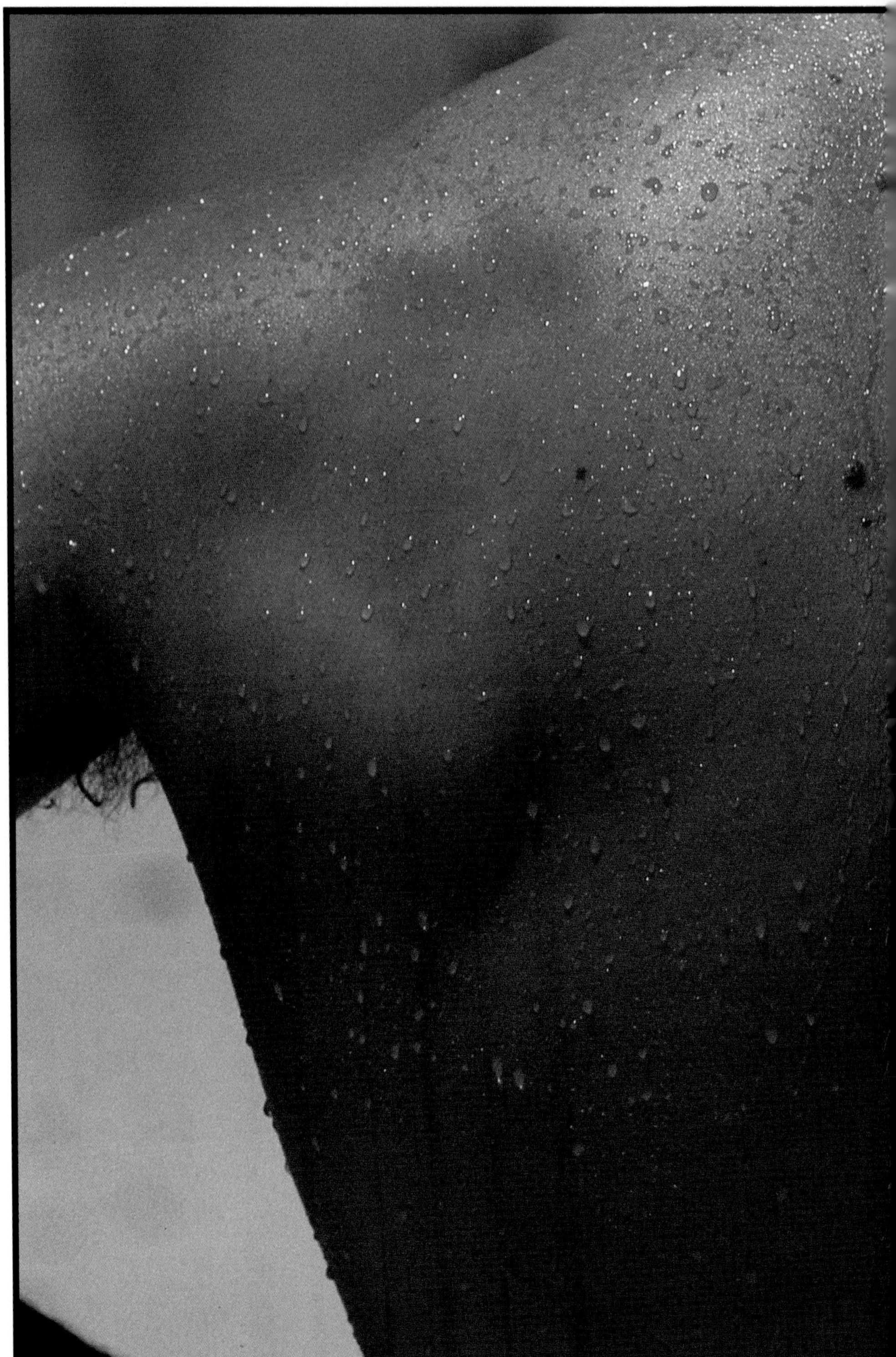

The lifesaving world continues to be dominated by the male, who is seen as hero of the beach by thousands of swimmers who trust in his skill and reliability.

Even when relaxing the life guard never forgets the motto of the Life Saving Association — Vigilance and Service. He constantly scans the water for those in trouble or other threats, such as sharks.

Although the traditional methods of rescue are still followed in the surf carnivals, they are being replaced by new, more advanced methods on the Australian beaches. Fast power-boats and inflatables get to a drowning person quicker than the surf boats and helicopters aid the search for swimmers in distress.

Rolling up his costume against slipping, each lifesaver prepares for competition.

With the competition over, the lifesavers relax.

A bronzed life guard casts a final respectful glance at the sea, his constant adversary in the battle to save lives on Australia's golden coastline.